Active Learning Calculus
Volume III

Derivatives and Applications

Mami Wentworth
Mel Henriksen
Emma Smith Zbarsky
Gary Simundza

Contents

Unit 5: Derivative Rules   **5**
    Unit 5-1: Chain Rule 7
    Unit 5-2: Product Rule 15
    Unit 5-3: Quotient Rule 21

Unit 6: Related Rates   **29**
    Unit 6-1: Implicit Differentiation 31
    Unit 6-2: Related Rates 37

Unit 7: Optimization   **49**
    Unit 7-1: Optimization 51
    Unit 7-2: Graphical Understanding 59

August 2022

Unit 5

Derivative Rules

5-1: Chain Rule
5-2: Product Rule
5-3: Quotient Rule

Unit 5-1: Chain Rule

Learning Outcomes

- Define, discuss, and interpret the concept of the derivative analytically, verbally, numerically, and graphically.

Overview

In this unit, we will explore techniques for differentiating more complex functions than those that we have addressed thus far. In this lesson, we will learn how to differentiate composite functions. In subsequent lessons, we will learn to differentiate products and quotients of functions.

A composite function is one that's made up of two or more simple functions. The table below shows several examples of composite functions as well as the simpler, basic functions that they contain.

Composite function	Component functions
$y(x) = \sin(3x)$	$\sin(x), 3x$
$y(t) = e^{\cos(t)}$	$e^t, \cos(t)$
$y(x) = (5x^2 + 3)^3$	$x^3, 5x^2 + 3$
$y(x) = \sqrt{\ln(x)}$	$\sqrt{x}, \ln(x)$

The composite function is "assembled" from its component functions in the way that's illustrated in Figure 1. One key to differentiating composite functions is decomposing them into their component functions. We will review that task below.

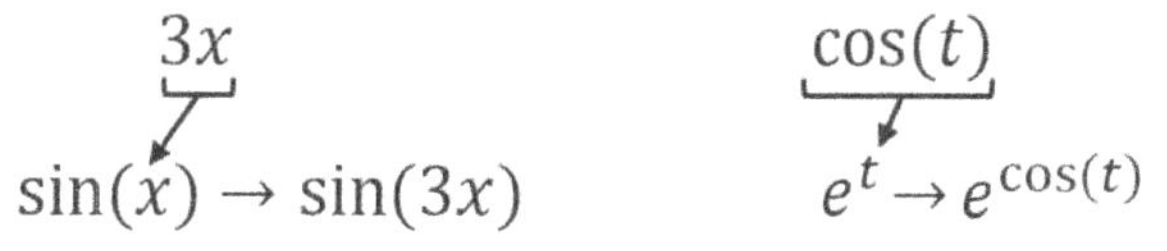

$$\sin(\overset{3x}{x}) \to \sin(3x) \qquad e^{\overset{\cos(t)}{t}} \to e^{\cos(t)}$$

Figure 1

1 Composite Functions and their Component Functions

Consider the first example function above, $y(x) = \sin(3x)$. This function is comprised of two simpler component functions which we identified in the table above. However, now we will designate these two functions $f(g)$ and $g(x)$ as shown in Figure 2 below.

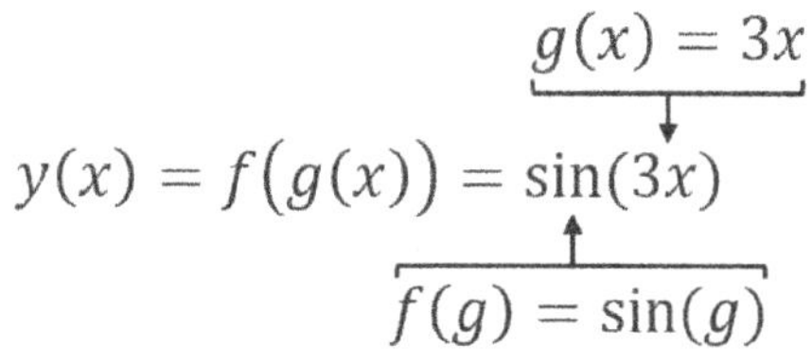

$$y(x) = f(g(x)) = \sin(3x)$$

with $g(x) = 3x$ and $f(g) = \sin(g)$.

Figure 2

1. Identify the component functions of the following composite functions.

Composite function	Component function	Component function
$y(x) = f(g(x))$	$f(g)$	$g(x)$
$y(x) = e^{\cos(x)}$		
$y(x) = (5x^2 + 3)^3$		
$y(x) = \sqrt{\ln(x)}$		
$y(x) = e^{3x+4}$		

2 Differentiating Composite Functions: The Chain Rule

A second key concept of differentiating composite functions is multiplying rates of change of the component functions. As a manager, your bonus increases at a rate three times the rate of your colleague's bonus. If your colleague's bonus increases by $5,000/year, consider the rate at which your bonus increases.

The rate of change of your bonus	=	The rate of change of your bonus with respect your colleague's bonus	$\cdot$	The rate at which your colleague's bonus increases
$\dfrac{d(\text{Your bonus})}{dt}$	=	$\dfrac{d(\text{Your bonus})}{d(\text{Colleague's bonus})}$	$\cdot$	$\dfrac{d(\text{Colleague's bonus})}{dt}$

Therefore, the rate at which your bonus increases is $3 \cdot \$5,000 = \$15,000$. In this way, the rate of change of a composite function involves multiplication of rates of change of component functions.

2. Consider the function $y(x) = \sin(3x)$. We have already learned in Unit 4-3 that

$$\frac{d}{dx}\sin(3x) = 3\cos(3x).$$

But we have seen previously that this is a composite function. Since we know what the derivative is from our previous study, let's see how we can discover a differentiation technique that can be used to arrive at this result.

We have seen above that we can decompose this function into its component functions:

$$y(x) = f(g(x)) = \sin(3x), \text{ where } f(g) = \sin(g) \text{ and } g(x) = 3x.$$

Let's differentiate the component functions. Substitute $3x$ for $g(x)$ in your final result for the derivative of $y(x)$.

$$\frac{dy(x)}{dx} = \frac{df(g)}{dg} \cdot \frac{dg(x)}{dx} = \boxed{} \cdot \boxed{}$$
$$\uparrow \qquad \uparrow$$
$$\frac{df(g)}{dg} \qquad \frac{dg(x)}{dx}$$

$$\frac{dy(x)}{dx} = \boxed{}$$

Note that these terms are the factors of the derivative of $y(x) = f(g(x)) = \sin(3x)$. This is illustrated below.

$$\frac{d\,y(x)}{dx} = \frac{d\sin(3x)}{dx} = \cos(3x) \cdot 3$$
$$\uparrow \qquad \uparrow$$
$$\frac{d\,y(x)}{dx} = \frac{d\,f(g(x))}{dx} = \frac{d\,f(g)}{d\!\!\!/g} \cdot \frac{d\!\!\!/g}{dx} = \frac{d\,f(g)}{dx}$$

Although derivatives are not fractions, they are limits of fractions and so, in many instances, we can treat them as fractions as we have done above. By taking the product of the derivatives of the two component functions, and "canceling out" the dg terms, we see that the product $\frac{df(g)}{dg} \cdot \frac{dg(x)}{dx}$ is equivalent to $\frac{dy(x)}{dx}$, the derivative of the composite function. The terms $\frac{df}{dg}$ and $\frac{dg}{dx}$ are *links* in the *chain* of factors that we have used to calculate the derivative of the composite function. This method of finding derivatives of composite functions is called the *chain rule*.

Because the product of the links of the chain (that is, the derivatives of the component functions) simplify to the derivative of the composite function, we can generalize this technique to other composite functions.

3. Consider the function $y(x) = e^{\cos(x)}$. Previously, we found that we can decompose this function as follows. Find the derivatives of the component functions.

- $f(g) = e^g$ $\qquad \dfrac{df}{dg} = \boxed{}$

- $g(x) = \cos(x)$ $\qquad \dfrac{dg}{dx} = \boxed{}$

Assemble a chain of derivative terms to find the derivative of $e^{\cos(x)}$. The final result should be a function of x.

$$\dfrac{dy(x)}{dx} = \dfrac{df}{dg} \cdot \dfrac{dg}{dx}$$

$$\dfrac{dy(x)}{dx} = \boxed{} \cdot \boxed{} = \boxed{}$$

4. Consider the remaining two composite functions that we looked at earlier. Rewrite the component functions, the derivative links of the chain rule and finally, the derivative of the composite function.

(a) $y = (5x^2 + 3)^3$

- $f(g) = \boxed{}$ $\qquad \dfrac{df}{dg} = \boxed{}$

- $g(x) = \boxed{}$ $\qquad \dfrac{dg}{dx} = \boxed{}$

$$\dfrac{dy(x)}{dx} = \dfrac{df}{dg} \cdot \dfrac{dg}{dx}$$

$$= \boxed{} \cdot \boxed{} = \boxed{}$$

(b) $f(x) = \sqrt{\ln(x)}$

- $f(g) = \boxed{}$ $\qquad \dfrac{df}{dg} = \boxed{}$

- $g(x) = \boxed{}$ $\qquad \dfrac{dg}{dx} = \boxed{}$

$$\dfrac{df(x)}{dx} = \dfrac{df}{dg} \cdot \dfrac{dg}{dx}$$

$$= \boxed{} \cdot \boxed{} = \boxed{}$$

3 Practice Using the Chain Rule

5. Use the chain rule to find the derivatives of the following composite functions.

   (a) $y(t) = \left(\sqrt{e^{5t}}\right)^3 = \left(e^{5t}\right)^{\frac{3}{2}}$

   (b) $y(x) = e^{(3x^2+2x+1)}$

   (c) $x(t) = \sin(\ln(t))$

   (d) $f(x) = \ln(\ln(3x))$

   (e) $y(x) = \cos^3(x^2)$

4 An Alternative Way of Thinking about the Chain Rule

Consider the function $y(x) = \cos(x^2)$. Let's consider the cosine function the "outer" function and x^2 the "inner" function. We can then say that the derivative of $\cos(x^2)$ is equal to the derivative of the outer function times the derivative of the inner function. This is illustrated in the figure below where we have used Lagrange (prime) notation to indicate the derivatives of the outer and inner functions. The inner function may also be thought of as the *argument* of the outer function.

$$\frac{d\cos(x^2)}{dx} = (\text{outer})' \cdot (\text{inner})' = -\sin(x^2) \cdot 2x = -2x\sin(x^2)$$

$$= \frac{d\,f(g)}{dg} \cdot \frac{dg}{dx}$$

Note that the derivatives of the outer and inner functions correspond to the "links" in the "chain" of the chain rule.

You might also think about this process as though you were evaluating a function with a simple calculator. To evaluate the example above at $x = 2$ you might first evaluate x^2 at $x = 2$ by entering 2^2. Then, to evaluate $\cos(x^2)$, you might enter $\cos(4)$. The first operation is with the "inner" function and the second, the "outer" function.

6. Differentiate the following composite functions by considering the outer and inner functions.

   (a) $y(t) = \cos(e^{3t})$

   (b) $y(x) = \sin^2(x)$

   (c) $s(x) = (4x^2 + 5x)^5$

5 An Application of the Chain Rule

7. The chair lift at the White Heat ski trail at Sunday River Skie Area in Maine moves at 5 meters per second over a total distanace of 1117 horizontal meters as it rises vertically 394 meters. How fast is a chair on the lift rising vertically?

(a) Using the figure below, fill in the boxes.

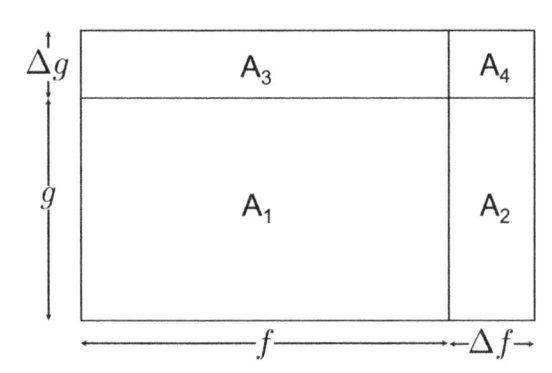

$$A(x + \Delta x) = (f + \Delta f)(g + \Delta g)$$
$$= A_1 + A_2 + A_3 + A_4$$
$$= \boxed{} + \boxed{} + \boxed{} + \boxed{}$$

(b) The change in the area is the difference between the new area and the original area:

$$\Delta A = A(x + \Delta x) - A$$
$$= (f \cdot g) + (\Delta f \cdot g) + (f \cdot \Delta g) + (\Delta f \cdot \Delta g) - (f \cdot g)$$
$$= \boxed{} + \boxed{} + \boxed{}$$

(c) The rate of change of the area is the following:

$$\frac{dA}{dx} = \lim_{\Delta x \to 0} \frac{\Delta A}{\Delta x}$$
$$= \lim_{\Delta x \to 0} \frac{(\Delta f \cdot g) + (f \cdot \Delta g) + (\Delta f \cdot \Delta g)}{\Delta x}$$

split the fraction into three fractions

$$= \lim_{\Delta x \to 0} \left(\boxed{} \; g + f \; \boxed{} + \boxed{} \right)$$

$$= g \cdot \lim_{\Delta x \to 0} \boxed{} + f \cdot \lim_{\Delta x \to 0} \boxed{} + \lim_{\Delta x \to 0} \boxed{}$$

(d) Now we consider the following limits:

- $\displaystyle\lim_{\Delta x \to 0} \frac{\Delta f}{\Delta x} = \boxed{}$

- $\displaystyle\lim_{\Delta x \to 0} \frac{\Delta g}{\Delta x} = \boxed{}$

- $\displaystyle\lim_{\Delta x \to 0} \frac{\Delta f \Delta g}{\Delta x} = \lim_{\Delta x \to 0} \frac{\Delta f}{\Delta x} \cdot \lim_{\Delta x \to 0} \Delta g = \boxed{} \cdot \boxed{} = \boxed{}$

Note: Recall that $\Delta g = g(x + \Delta x) - g(x)$.

Therefore,
$$\frac{dA}{dx} = \frac{d}{dx}(f \cdot g) = \frac{df}{dx} \cdot g + f \cdot \frac{dg}{dx}$$

In the Lagrange notation,
$$(f \cdot g)' = f' \cdot g + f \cdot g'$$

This is called the *Product Rule* for differentiation.

Product Rule:

$$(f \cdot g)' = f' \cdot g + f \cdot g'$$

$$\frac{d}{dx}(f \cdot g) = \frac{df}{dx} \cdot g + f \cdot \frac{dg}{dx}$$

3 Spaghetti Experiment Revisited

Recall in Unit 4-2, we looked at the spaghetti oscillation. The displacement data were modeled with a sine function without consideration for the decreasing amplitude as in Figure 1 (i). It turns out that the amplitude can be adjusted by making the amplitude, C_1, a function of t (ie. $C_2 e^{kt}$). The data can better be modeled with the function of the form as seen in Figure 1 (ii). The green curves are called the *envelope* of the sine function: $y = \pm C_2 e^{kt}$; they are the changing amplitude of the oscillation. Here, we used the values $C_1 = 1.45$, $C_2 = 1.62$, $k = -1$, $\omega = 55.1$ and $\phi = -2.26$. Figure 1 contains more data points than what we used previously for clarity.

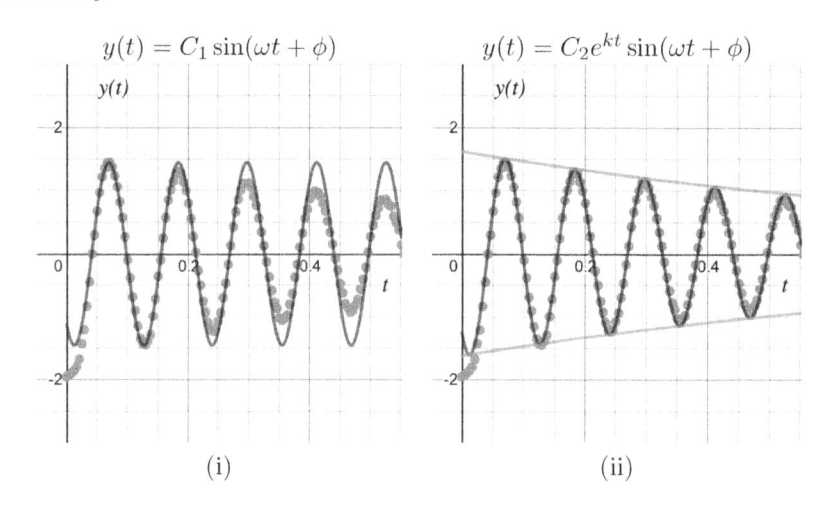

Figure 1: Spaghetti oscillation displacement data fitted with two functions.

2. What are $f(t)$ and $g(t)$ such that $y(t) = f(t) \cdot g(t)$ for the displacement function?
$$y(t) = 1.62 e^{-t} \sin(55.1t - 2.26)$$

3. Find $f'(t)$ and $g'(t)$.

4. Use the product rule to find $\dfrac{d}{dt} y(t) = \dfrac{d}{dt}(f \cdot g)$.

3.1 Average Velocity Data

By now, we have computed the derivatives of the functions that were fitted to the displacement data. The velocity function found in Unit 4-2 and the velocity function we found in the previous problem in this lesson are plotted in Figure 2 (i) and (ii), respectively.

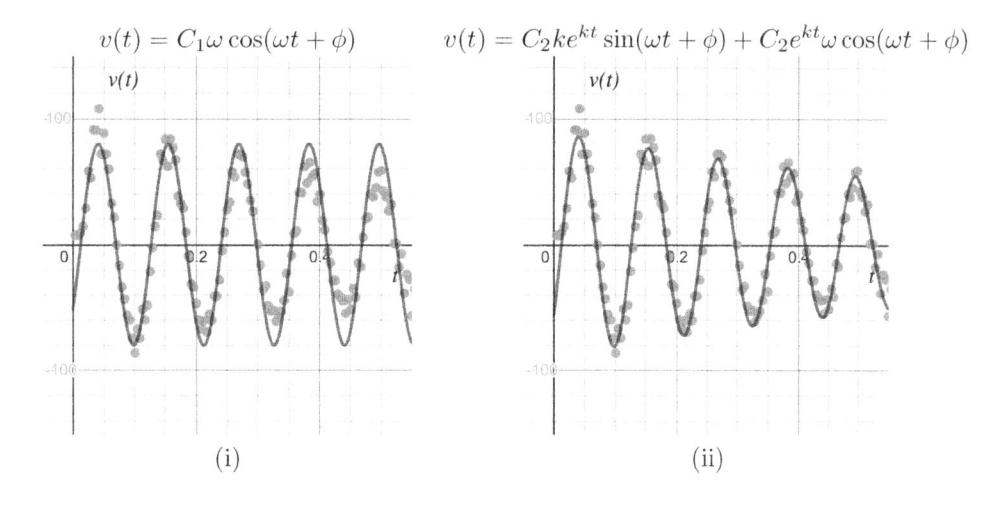

$$v(t) = C_1 \omega \cos(\omega t + \phi) \qquad v(t) = C_2 k e^{kt} \sin(\omega t + \phi) + C_2 e^{kt} \omega \cos(\omega t + \phi)$$

(i)   (ii)

Figure 2: Spaghetti oscillation velocity data fitted with two functions.

5. Which velocity functions fit the velocity data better? Why?

4 Chain Rule and Product Rule

Differentiation of some functions involve more than one rule - one may have to employ any or all combinations of basic differentiation formulas, the chain rule and the product rule.

6. Identify the rules you have to use to differentiate the functions below. Then, differentiate them.

   (a) $y(t) = t^2 \cos(t)$

   (b) $y(t) = \dfrac{\sin(t)}{t^2} = \sin(t) \cdot t^{-2}$

   (c) $g(r) = 4e^{3(r-1)}(3r^3 + 2r^2 + 4r)$

   (d) $x(t) = \sin(3t+1)\cos(5t-1)$

   (e) $y(\theta) = \theta \cdot \sin^2(2\theta)$

Unit 5-3: Quotient Rule

Learning Outcomes

- Define, discuss, and interpret the concept of the derivative analytically, verbally, numerically, and graphically.

Overview

In Unit 5-2, we studied the Product Rule, which is applied to differentiate a product of functions of the form $y(t) = f(t) \cdot g(t)$. The product rule is:

$$\frac{d}{dt}(f \cdot g) = \frac{df}{dt} \cdot g + f \cdot \frac{dg}{dt}$$

In this lesson, we will study the Quotient Rule, which is applied to a quotient of functions of the form $y(t) = \frac{f(t)}{g(t)}$.

1 Quotient Rule

Similarly to the discussion of the product of functions in Unit 5-2, we will begin this lesson by discussing quotients of functions. Consider the following function: $y(t) = \frac{t^3 - t^2 + 4}{e^t}$. The function in the numerator we refer to as $f(t)$ whereas the function in the denominator we refer to as $g(t)$.

$$y(t) = \frac{\overbrace{t^3 - t^2 + 4}^{f(t)}}{\underbrace{e^t}_{g(t)}}$$

1. Follow the steps to develop a derivative rule to differentiate a quotient of functions, $y(t) = \frac{f(t)}{g(t)}$.

   (a) Write $\dfrac{1}{g(t)}$ as a term with a negative exponent.

   (b) Rewrite the expression as a product.

   $$y(t) = \frac{f(t)}{g(t)} = f \cdot \underbrace{\boxed{}}_{g_1(t)}$$

   (c) The derivative of f is $\dfrac{d}{dt}f = f'$. Differentiate g_1.

   $$\frac{d}{dt}g_1 = \frac{d}{dt}g^{-1} = \boxed{}$$

   (d) Write the derivative of $f \cdot g_1$ using the product rule, then substitute g_1' from (c).

   $$y'(t) = (f \cdot g_1)' = \boxed{}\boxed{} + \boxed{}\boxed{} = \boxed{}\boxed{} - \boxed{}\boxed{}$$

2. So far, we have $\frac{d}{dt}(f \cdot g^{-1}) = \frac{df}{dt} \cdot g^{-1} - f \cdot \left(g^{-2}\frac{dg}{dt}\right)$. We can simplify the right side in the following manner.

   (a) Rewrite the negative exponent in the denominator.

   $$\frac{d}{dt}(f \cdot g^{-1}) = \boxed{} \cdot \frac{1}{\boxed{}} - \boxed{} \cdot \frac{1}{\boxed{}} \cdot \boxed{}$$

   $$= \frac{\boxed{}}{\boxed{}} - \frac{\boxed{}}{\boxed{}}$$

   (b) Multiply $\frac{f'}{g}$ by $\frac{g}{g}$.

   $$\frac{d}{dt}(f \cdot g^{-1}) = \frac{\boxed{}}{\boxed{}} - \frac{\boxed{}}{\boxed{}}$$

   (c) Combine the two fractions with the common denominator, g^2.

   $$\frac{d}{dt}(f \cdot g^{-1}) = \frac{\boxed{} - \boxed{}}{\boxed{}}$$

   The result is the *Quotient Rule* for differentiation.

   Quotient Rule:
   $$\frac{d}{dt}\left(\frac{f}{g}\right) = \left(\frac{f}{g}\right)' = \frac{f'g - fg'}{g^2}$$

Note that the expression in the numerator of the quotient rule is a difference. Therefore, the order of subtraction matters. Unlike the product rule, the numerator of the quotient term, $f(t)$, must be differentiated first.

Some students like to refer to f and g as "top" and "bottom" functions. Others like to remember the correct order by referring to "high" and "low."

2 Combination of Differentiation Rules

3. Identify the differentiation rule(s) needed, then differentiate.

   (a) $f(\theta) = \tan(\theta)$

   (b) $x(t) = \dfrac{\sin(3t)}{\cos(5t)}$

   (c) $f(t) = \dfrac{t^2}{\cos(t)}$

   (d) $g(r) = \dfrac{4e^{3r}}{3r^3 + 2r^2 + 4r}$

3 Product Rule vs. Quotient Rule

The quotient rule, as the name suggests, is applied to a quotient of functions for differentiation. However, it is worth noting that *any* quotient can be expressed as a product as seen earlier in this lesson.

$$y(t) = \frac{f(t)}{g(t)} = f(t) \cdot (g(t))^{-1}$$

Thus, one can always use the product rule instead of the quotient rule. In fact, it is sometimes simpler to rewrite a quotient as a product before applying any differentiation rules.

4. Differentiate without using the quotient rule. Avoid the product rule if possible, and use correct notation for derivatives, equality, etc.

   (a) $\dfrac{d}{dt}\left(\dfrac{2}{t^3}\right)$

   (b) $\dfrac{d}{dx}\left(\dfrac{e^{2x}}{2e^{5x}}\right)$

   (c) $\dfrac{d}{ds}\left(\dfrac{4s^2 - 6s}{2s}\right)$

   (d) $\dfrac{d}{dt}\left(\dfrac{t^2}{\ln(5t)}\right)$

   (e) $\dfrac{d}{dr}\left(\dfrac{1}{\sqrt{r}}\right)$

4 Summary

5. Complete the following statements to summarize the key points from this unit.

   (a) **Chain Rule:** $\dfrac{d}{dt} f(g(t)) =$

   (b) **Product Rule:** $\dfrac{d}{dt}(f(t) \cdot g(t)) =$

   (c) **Quotient Rule:** $\dfrac{d}{dt} \dfrac{f(t)}{g(t)} =$

Unit 6

Related Rates

6-1: Implicit Differentiation
6-2: Related Rates

Unit 6-1: Implicit Differentiation

Learning Outcomes

- Find the derivatives of functions and of implicitly defined relations using differentiation rules.
- Model and solve related rates problems using derivatives.

Overview

In all of our discussions of derivatives and antiderivatives thus far, we have dealt with functions of the form $y = f(x)$. Below are a few examples of these types of functions. Note that in all of these examples, the dependent variable, y, is isolated on one side of the equation.

$$y = x^2 \qquad y = \cos(x) \qquad y = \sqrt{6x^3 + 2x}$$

$$y = 3x^2 + 5x \qquad y = \ln(5x+1) \qquad y = \frac{(x+5)^2}{x^3+1}$$

1 Implicit Functions and Relations

1. Now consider the relation:
$$x^2 + y^2 = 1 \tag{1}$$

   (a) ☐ Plot this relation in Desmos. This relation plots what figure?

   (b) Why do we refer to this as a relation and not a function?

   (c) What would you do to find the slope of the curve at any point? What features of this relation pose a problem to finding the slope compared to functions we have addressed up until now?

   (d) Solve the equation $x^2 + y^2 = 1$ for y. Recall that if $a^2 = b$ then $a = \pm\sqrt{b}$.

   (e) In Question 1d, we found two different functions. ☐ Plot these functions in Desmos.
   (f) Find expressions for the slope of the functions below at any point.

$$y = \sqrt{1-x^2} \tag{2}$$
$$y = -\sqrt{1-x^2} \tag{3}$$

The functions in Eqs. 2 and 3 are written *explicitly*, like the functions listed in the Overview. The relation in Eq. 1 is written *implicitly*, that is, the dependent variable is not isolated as it is in the explicit representation. We already know how to differentiate Eqs. 2 and 3, but there is no reason we cannot differentiate Eq. 1 as well.

2. In Question 1, we plotted the explicit and implicit representations of the unit circle. We found the derivative, $\frac{dy}{dx}$, in Question 1f by differentiating the explicit representation. We will now see how we can find $\frac{dy}{dx}$ using the implicit representation, $x^2 + y^2 = 1$. We will differentiate both sides of this relation in a series of steps.

$$\frac{d}{dx}(x^2 + y^2) = \frac{d}{dx}(1)$$

$$\frac{d}{dx}(x^2) + \frac{d}{dx}(y^2) = \frac{d}{dx}(1)$$

(a) Fill in the two boxes to the right begin the differentiation process.

(b) Recognizing that y^2 is a function of y, and y is a function of x, we can apply the chain rule to differentiate y^2 with respect to y and y with respect to x.

Fill in the four boxes appropriately to write the completed derivative equation.

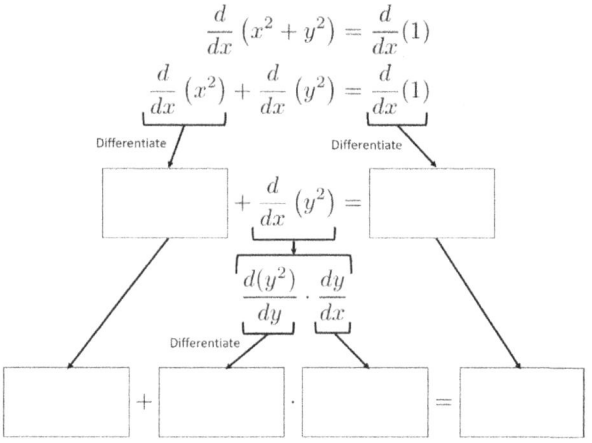

(c) Now solve the equation you found in Question 2b for $\frac{dy}{dx}$ to find the derivative of y.

$$\frac{dy}{dx} = \frac{\boxed{}}{\boxed{}}$$

(d) How does the result from Question 2c compare to the result from Question 1f? Keep in mind the result of Question 1d.

2 Further Exploration of Implicit Relations

In the previous section, we looked at the equation for the unit circle, $x^2 + y^2 = 1$. We saw that this is an implicit representation of the equation for the unit circle. We also saw that this relationship can be expressed as two functions: $y = \sqrt{1-x^2}$ and $y = -\sqrt{1-x^2}$.

Implicit differentiation may be used on a relation that can be expressed explicitly as an alternative to rewriting the expression. However, it is most powerful when used with relations that cannot be expressed explicitly. We will consider such a relation in this section.

3. Consider the relation below called the *Folium of Descartes*:

$$x^3 + y^3 = axy, \text{ where } a \text{ is a constant.}$$

Note that this relation cannot be expressed as an explicit function $y(x)$ or $x(y)$.

   (a) ☐ Plot this relation in Desmos for $a = 1$.

   (b) Find an expression for $\dfrac{dy}{dx}$ for this relation.

      i. Differentiate both sides of the equation:

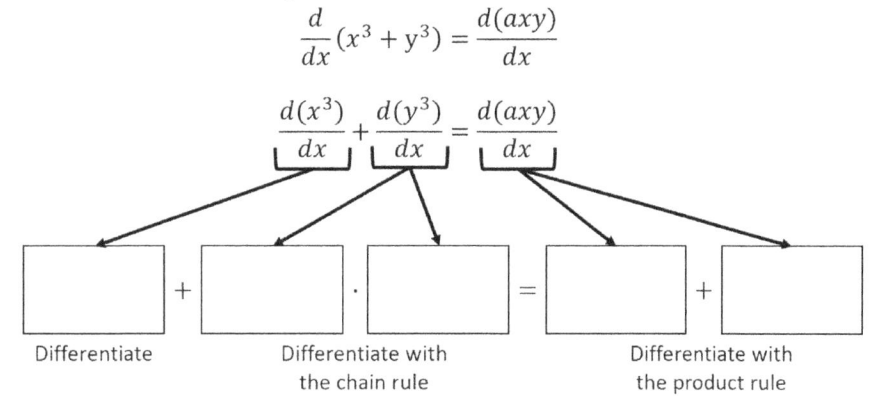

$$\frac{d}{dx}(x^3 + y^3) = \frac{d(axy)}{dx}$$

$$\underbrace{\frac{d(x^3)}{dx}} + \underbrace{\frac{d(y^3)}{dx}} = \underbrace{\frac{d(axy)}{dx}}$$

☐ + ☐ · ☐ = ☐ + ☐

Differentiate   Differentiate with   Differentiate with
                      the chain rule   the product rule

      ii. Solve for $\dfrac{dy}{dx}$.

   (c) For $a = 1$, find the points on the curve where the slope is zero.

(d) For $a = 1$, find the points on the curve where the slope is undefined.

(e) ☐ Check in Desmos that your answers to Questions 3c and 3d are reasonable.

3 Practicing Implicit Differentiation

4. Find an expression for the rate of change of y with respect to x for the following relations:

(a) $10x^4 - 18xy^2 + 10y^3 = 48$

(b) $x^2y + 5x^4y^2 = xy$

(c) $xe^y = 6xy + y^2$

(d) $e^{xy} = \cos(y^3)$

Active Learning Calculus   Unit 6-2: Related Rates   6-2-1

Unit 6-2: Related Rates

Learning Outcomes

- Find the derivatives of functions and of implicitly defined relations using differentiation rules.
- Model and solve related rates problems using derivatives.

Overview

Thus far, we've discussed rates of change and characterized the derivative of a function as the rate at which that function changes with respect to its independent variable. In this lesson, we will look at equations that involve two different rates of change.

Many situations exhibit multiple rates of change that are related to one another. We will look at several such examples in this lesson and employ the chain rule and implicit differentiation to develop the relationships between these rates of change.

1 Introduction to Related Rates

1. Suppose we are adding water to fill a cylindrically shaped above ground pool as pictured in Figure 1. We do not want to waste time watching the pool fill. Instead, we would like to calculate the time it will take to fill the pool based on the rate of flow of water into the pool. Note that the rate at which the water flows into the pool is the same as the rate of change of the volume of water in the pool, $\dfrac{dV}{dt}$.

   We have drawn a sketch of the pool in the right side of Figure 1 and labeled the relevant quantities.

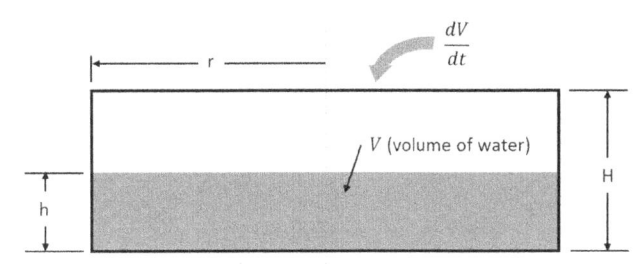

   Figure 1: Cylindrical Pool

   (a) Which of the quantities listed in the table below (and shown in Figure 1) are changing with time? Indicate "Yes" or "No" in the table and explain your reasoning.

Quantity	Changes with time?	Explain your reasoning
V		
H		
h		
r		
$\dfrac{dV}{dt}$		

37

(b) Write an equation that relates V and h.

$$V = \boxed{} h$$

(c) Note that the equation we wrote in Question 1b does not involve time. Also, we suspect that the quantity $\dfrac{dV}{dt}$ is somehow connected to the rate at which the water level rises, $\dfrac{dh}{dt}$.

How can we transform the equation we wrote in Question 1b into one that relates $\dfrac{dV}{dt}$ and $\dfrac{dh}{dt}$?

(d) Differentiate the left and right sides of the equation we wrote in Question 1b with respect to time. Use implicit differentiation to differentiate the right side. The quantity h is changing with time so we will express that rate of change as $\dfrac{dh}{dt}$.

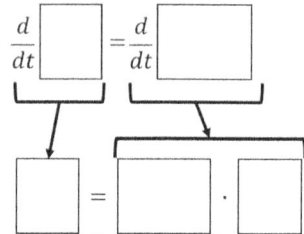

$$\dfrac{d}{dt}\boxed{} = \dfrac{d}{dt}\boxed{}$$

$$\boxed{} = \boxed{} \cdot \boxed{}$$

(e) Solve the equation you developed in Question 1d to find the rate at which the height will change with time, $\dfrac{dh}{dt}$, in terms of the other quantities. Assume that $\dfrac{dV}{dt} = 6$ gallons/min $= 1386$ in^3/min, and $r = 72$ inches.

(f) Find the time it takes to fill the pool to a height of 30 inches.

Key concepts from this problem:

- Problems involving relationships between two rates of change are called *related rates* problems.
- The equation we wrote in Question 1b that relates volume to height is called a *static* equation, because the quantities it relates are not rates of change.
- The equation we wrote in Question 1d, however, relates two rates of change and is called a *dynamic* equation.
- The process of solving related rates problems typically has these steps:
  1. Make a sketch of the problem, labeling the various quantities and identifying which are changing.
  2. Write a static equation
  3. Differentiate both sides to arrive at a dynamic equation.
  4. Solve the dynamic equation for the quantity of interest.

2 Rate of Change of the Height of a Conical Sand Pile

2. Consider a dump truck dumping sand from a single small portal at the rear of the truck bed. The sand spills into a cone-shaped mound on the ground behind the truck. The ratio of height to base is maintained as the pouring sand increases the size of the cone. We have drawn a sketch of the situation in Figure 2 labeled with the relevant quantities.

   Find the rate at which the height h of the cone is changing with time, $\dfrac{dh}{dt}$, when the height of the pile is 6 feet. Note that this rate will be a function of the rate at which sand flows onto the conical sand pile, $\dfrac{dV}{dt}$. When the sand pile has radius R, the height is H.

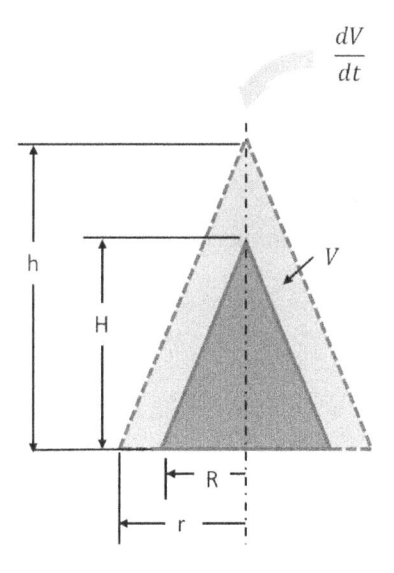

   Figure 2: Sand Pile

   (a) Identify and list the various quantities and state whether or not they are changing with time.

(b) Now write a static equation relating the volume of sand in the conical pile, V, to the height of the pile, h. Feel free to look up the volume of a cone if you need to.

(c) The volume of the sand pile changes with both r and h. We must eliminate one of these quantities from the static equation before we differentiate. Write an equation that relates these two quantities to one another. Specifically, write r in terms of h.

(d) Using the relationship you found between r and h, rewrite the static equation so that V is dependent only on the variable h.

(e) Differentiate the left side of the equation you found in Question 2d to find the rate of change of volume with respect to time.
$$\boxed{} = \frac{d}{dt}\left(\frac{\pi\left(\frac{R}{H}\right)^2 h^3}{3}\right)$$

(f) Differentiate the right side of the equation using the chain rule and implicit differentiation knowing that $h = f(t)$.
$$\frac{dV}{dt} = \boxed{} \cdot \frac{dh}{dt}$$

(g) Solve for $\dfrac{dh}{dt}$.

(h) Assuming the following values, find $\dfrac{dh}{dt}$ when $h = 6$ feet.

$$H = 3 \text{ ft.}$$
$$R = 2.5 \text{ ft.}$$
$$\frac{dV}{dt} = 15 \text{ ft.}^3 \text{ per min.}$$

3 Rate of Change of Water Height in a Spherical Vase

3. In this part of the lesson, we will again take a look at the rate of increase of the depth of water in a container in relation to a constant rate of water poured into that container. However, in this case, the container will be a spherical flower vase as pictured in Figure 3. For the purpose of this analysis, we will idealize the vase as a complete sphere (without the flat bottom).

Figure 3: Spherical flower vase

(a) It's helpful to first draw a sketch of the problem, in this case the vase, and label these relevant quantities:
- $\dfrac{dV}{dt}$ - The rate of change of volume with time
- V - The volume of water in the vase
- R - The radius of the sphere
- h - The depth of the water in the vase

(b) Identify which quantities are changing with time and which are constants.

(c) Determine what two variables we need to relate to each other and write the static equation by defining their relationship. (Hint: find a formula for the volume of a "spherical cap.")

(d) ☐ Plot the volume function in Desmos. Assume that $R = 3$. Limit the domain of the function appropriately. Discuss with your group if this plot makes sense, that is, does it describe what you intuitively expect will happen to the water level as you add water at a constant rate.

(e) Find the dynamic equation by differentiating the static equation with respect to time.

(f) Solve for the rate of change of the water height in terms of the rate of change of volume.

(g) ☐ Plot in Desmos the function describing the rate of change of water height with respect to water volume. Assume that $\frac{dV}{dt} = 1$ and $R = 3$. Limit the domain of the function appropriately.

(h) Discuss with your group if this plot makes sense. Does it describe what you intuitively expect will happen to the rate of change of the water level as you add water at a constant rate? Record key points of your discussion below.

4 Summary

4. List the possible steps to follow in solving a problem involving two related rates of change.

Unit 7

Optimization

7-1: Optimization
7-2: Graphical Understanding

Unit 7-1: Optimization

Learning Outcomes

- Model and solve optimization problems using derivatives.

Overview

In this unit, we will study problems that involve finding minima or maxima of a given function. This type of problem is called an *optimization* problem.

1 Maximizing the Volume of a Box

1. Make an open-topped box using a sheet of paper (11" x 8.5", copy paper) by cutting out equal-sized squares from each of the four corners and folding the paper on the dotted lines shown in Figure 1. Select a length for the side of the cut-out, x, so that the box you form will have the largest possible enclosed volume.

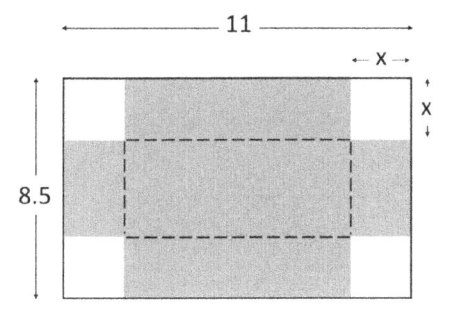

Figure 1: A square is removed from each of the corners to make an open box.

(a) Write the dimensions of your box and the volume in terms of the length x.

(b) Explain why you chose the dimensions like you did.

2 Graphical Solution

The function for which we are trying to find minima or maxima is called an *objective function*.

2. (a) Write the objective function for our volume maximizing problem.
$$V(x) =$$

(b) Graph the objective function in Desmos. Sketch the graph below.

3. (a) What is the maximum volume, $V_{\max}$?

(b) What is the value, x_0, at which the max volume occurs?

(c) What is the slope of the function at the point $(x_0, V_{\max})$?

4. Explain how you used the graph to determine the max volume and the value of x at which the volume is a maximum.

3 Analytical Solution

5. Referring to the graph you sketched in the previous problem, what can you say about the derivative of the objective function at the maximum point?

6. (a) Differentiate the objective function.

   (b) Set the derivative of the objective function equal to zero, and find the solution.

   (c) What does the solution represent?

   (d) Find the maximum volume.

7. (a) Find the second derivative of the objective function.

   (b) Evaluate the second derivative at the point that maximizes the volume.

   (c) What does the sign of the second derivative tell us?

8. Summarize how you used the derivative to determine the maximum volume and the value of x, where the maximum volume occurs.

Active Learning Calculus Unit 7-1: Optimization 7-1-5

4 Application

A standard soda can holds 12 oz. of liquid. Let's explore why soda cans are shaped the way they are.

9. What factors do you think affected the decision to settle on the shape you see in stores?

10. Suppose that a can manufacturer wants to produce a 355 mL (12 oz.) can. The manufacturer wants to minimize the surface area of the material used to make cans. Assume that the whole can is made of a single material. For simplicity, assume that the can is a perfect cylinder.

   (a) What is the physical interpretation of the surface area? Why are we interested in minimizing the surface area?

   (b) Write the objective function for the can problem. Use h for the height and r for the radius of the cylinder. Make sure to specify whether you are minimizing or maximizing.

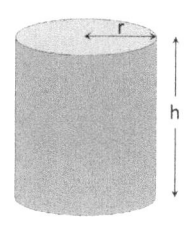

   (c) Write the *constraint equation* for the problem. The constraints provide a relationship between multiple variables used in the objective function.

   (d) Rewrite the objective function in terms of a single variable using the constraint equation.

11. We will find the solution to the optimization problem analytically.

    (a) Differentiate the objective function.

    (b) Set the derivative of the objective function equal to 0 and find the solution.

    (c) What does the solution represent?

12. What are the dimensions of the can that has the minimum surface area given the set volume of 12 oz.?

13. (a) Use the second derivative to determine that the point you found is indeed a minimum.

    (b) Graph the objective function and verify your answer to the previous problem.

14. (a) How do the optimal dimensions compare to the actual dimensions of a standard can?

    (b) Why are the optimized dimensions and the actual dimensions different?

Unit 7-2: Graphical Understanding of Derivatives

Learning Outcomes

- Model and solve optimization problems using derivatives.

Overview

We have discussed minima and maxima in the context of optimization in Unit 7-1. In this lesson, we will take a closer look into extrema (min/max) and other *critical points*, where the derivative of the function is either zero or does not exist. We will study the relationship between first and second derivatives, and what these derivatives tell us about the graph of a function.

1 Local and Absolute Extrema

Consider the soda optimization problem we solved in Unit 7-1. Given the fixed volume of 355 mL, we wanted to minimize the surface area of the can. Take a look at the surface area function for the soda can.:

$$S(x) = 2\pi x h + 2\pi r^2 = \frac{710}{x} + 2\pi x^2$$

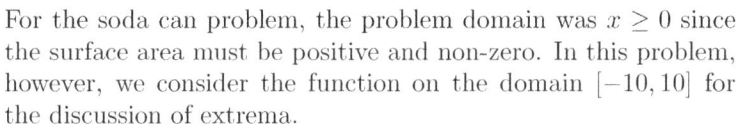

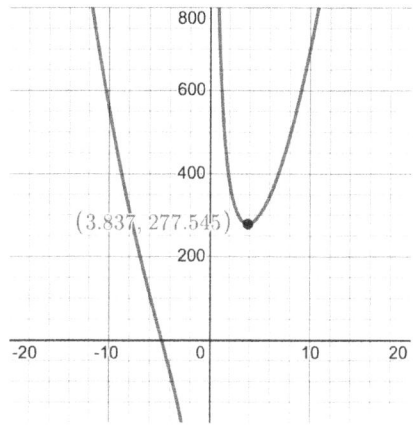

For the soda can problem, the problem domain was $x \geq 0$ since the surface area must be positive and non-zero. In this problem, however, we consider the function on the domain $[-10, 10]$ for the discussion of extrema.

We can see that the slope at $x_0 = 3.837$ is zero. A point where the derivative is zero is called a *critial point*. Below are several notes about critical points.

- A point at which the slope of the function is undefined is also called a *critical point*.

- A minimum or a maximum occurs at a critical point.
    - A critical point is a *local minimum* if the function value at the point is lower than the points around it.
    - A critical point is an *absolute minimum* (or global minimum) if the function value at that point is lower than *all* the points in the given domain.
    - A critical point is a *local maximum* if the function value at the point is higher than the points around it.
    - A critical point is an *absolute maximum* (or global maximum) if the function value at that point is higher than *all* the points in the given domain.

- A critical point may not necessarily be a minimum or a maximum.

1. Consider the domain $[-10, 10]$ on the graph. Is the point $(3.837, 277.545)$ a local minimum, an absolute minimum, or both? Explain your reasoning.

2. Consider the function defined on $[0, 3.5]$ and graphed below.

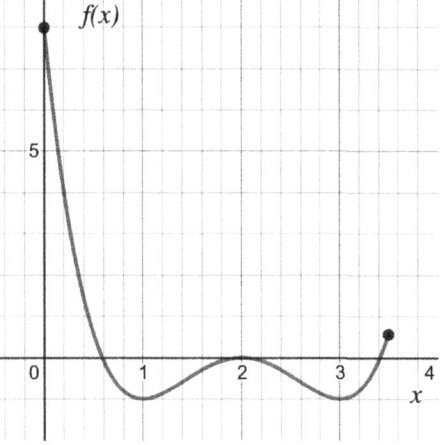

    (a) Find all the x values where the local minima occur, and find the associated values of the minima.

    (b) Find all the x values where the local maxima occur, and find the associated values of the maxima.

    (c) Find the absolute minimum.

    (d) Find the absolute maximum.

2 First Derivatives: Increasing and Decreasing Functions

3. Consider the function below. Let's explore the first derivative of the function. Three local extrema are marked with ×.

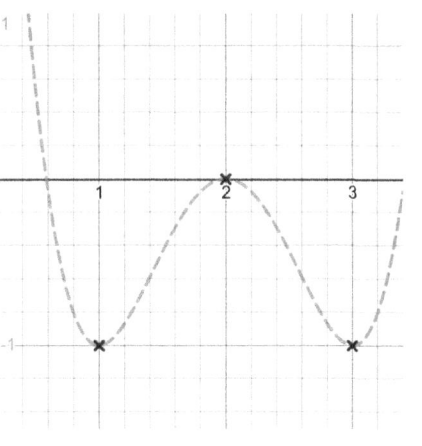

    (a) Trace the portions of the function where the function is increasing.

    (b) Where the function is increasing, the rate of change of the function (ie. the first derivative of the function) is *positive / negative*. (Circle the correct term.)

    (c) Trace the portions of the function (with a different color) where the function is decreasing.

    (d) Where the function is decreasing, the rate of change of the function (ie. the first derivative of the function) is *positive / negative*. (Circle the correct term.)

3 Second Derivatives: Concavity and Inflection Points

The concept of *concavity* was introduced briefly in Unit 3-2. Concavity tells us whether the function is valley-shaped or mountain-shaped.

- When the function opens upward, we call it *concave up*, whereas when the function opens downward, we call it *concave down*.

- The point at which the concavity changes is called an *inflection point*.

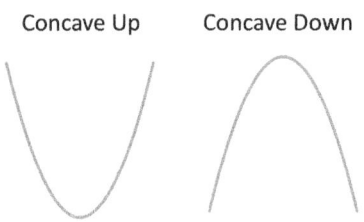

4. Consider the function below. Let's explore the second derivative of the function. Two inflection points are marked with ×.

    (a) Trace the pieces of the function where the function is concave up.

    (b) Where the function is concave up, the slope changes from very negative to slightly negative to zero to slightly positive to very positive. In this case, the rate of change of slope (ie. the second derivative of the function) is *positive / negative*. (Circle the correct term.)

    (c) Trace the piece of the function (with a different color) where the function is concave down.

    (d) Where the function is concave down, the slope changes from very positive to zero to negative. In this case, the rate of change of slope (ie. the second derivative of the function) is *positive / negative*. (Circle the correct term.)

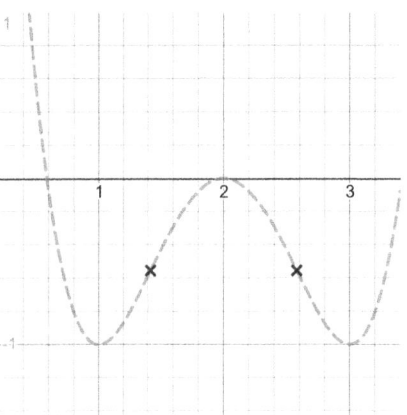

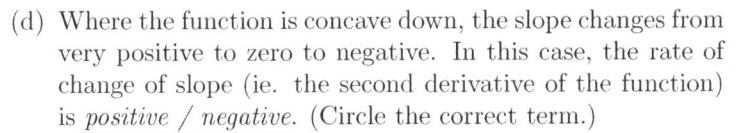

5. Complete the table below and summarize what the first and the second derivatives of the function tell us about the function.

	Sign	Information about the function, $f(x)$
First Derivative	$f'(x) > 0$	
	$f'(x) < 0$	
Second Derivative	$f''(x) > 0$	
	$f''(x) < 0$	

4 Relationship between First and Second Derivatives

Suppose that a car is moving in a straight line. We've discussed before that the rate of change of displacement is *velocity*. Now, the rate of change of velocity is called *acceleration*. This implies that the acceleration is the first derivative of velocity and the second derivative of displacement.

$$\text{Displacement: } p(t)$$
$$\text{Velocity: } v(t) = p'(t)$$
$$\text{Acceleration: } a(t) = v'(t) = p''(t)$$

Positive acceleration means the car is speeding up in the forward direction or slowing down going backward whereas a negative acceleration means the car is slowing down going forward or speeding up going backward.

4.1 Displacement from Velocity

6. Consider the following velocity graph of a car moving in a straight line. Describe in words how the car is moving (speeding up or slowing down) in what direction (forward or backward) between 0 and 22 seconds.

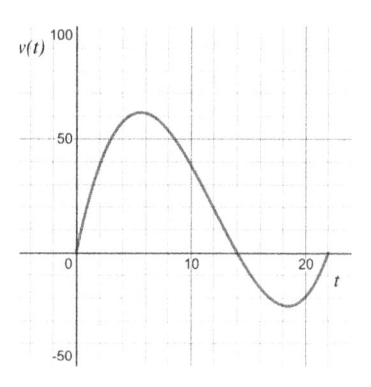

7. Which of the following graphs best represents the displacement between $[0, 14]$? What about $[14, 22]$? Explain your reasoning.

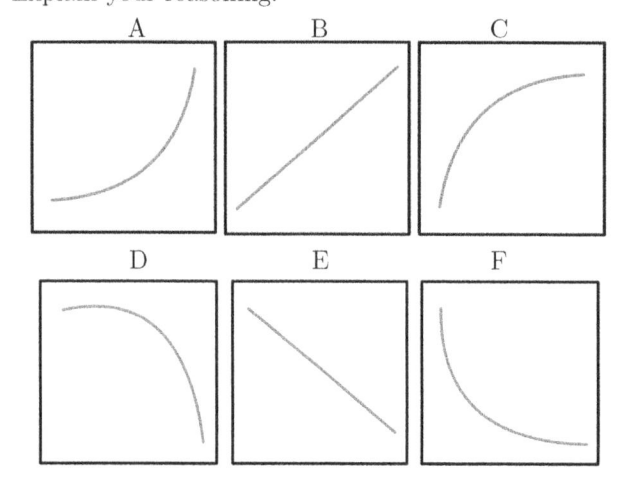

8. Sketch the displacement based on your answers to the previous questions.

4.2 Acceleration from Velocity

9. Next, we consider acceleration from velocity.

   (a) List all points where the acceleration is zero.

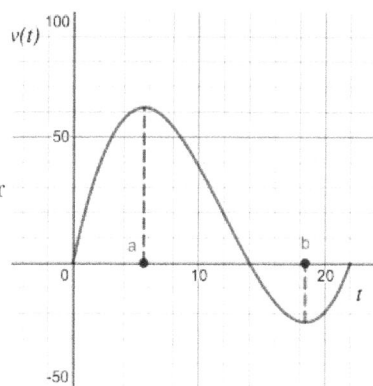

   (b) List the interval(s) in which the acceleration is positive or negative.
   - Positive Acceleration:
   - Negative Acceleration:

   (c) Sketch the acceleration based on your answers to the previous questions.

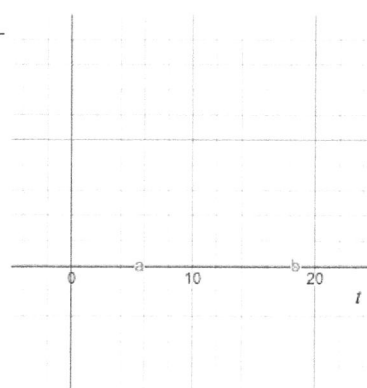

10. Consider the three functions, $p(t)$, $v(t)$ and $a(t)$, graphed on the right.

- What is the significant characteristic of each of the functions at $t = a$?

- What is the significant characteristic of each of the functions at $t = b$?

- On the interval(s) in which $p(t)$ is concave down, what can you say about the slope of $v(t)$ and about the function value of $a(t)$?

- On the interval(s) in which $p(t)$ is concave up, what can you say about the slope of $v(t)$ and about the function value of $a(t)$?

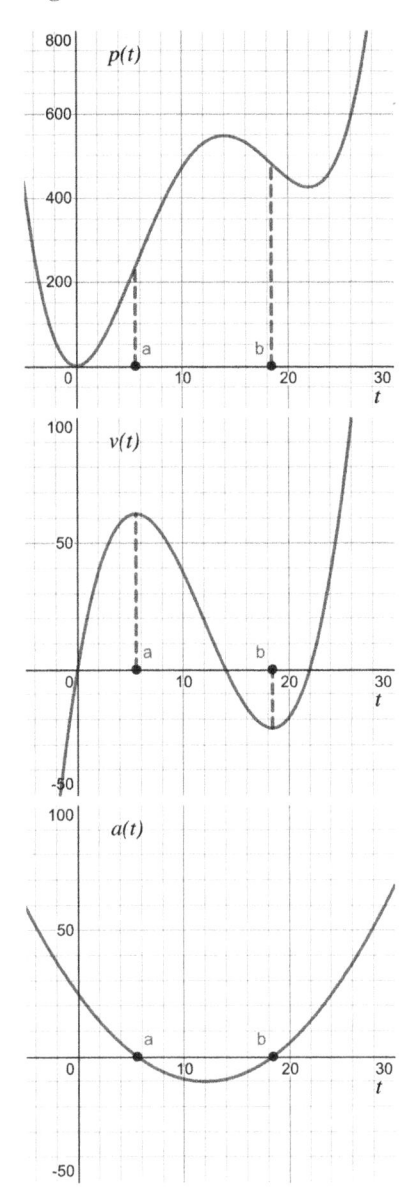

5 Using Second Derivatives to Characterize Extrema

We discussed that the sign of the second derivative tells us whether the function is concave up or concave down. At an inflection point, we saw that the second derivative is zero. Using the second derivative to determine whether the critical point is a minimum or a maximum is called the *Second Derivative Test*. However, a zero second derivative <u>does not</u> necessarily imply an inflection point.

Second Derivative Test

Let x_0 be a critical point of $f(x)$.

- If $f''(x_0) > 0$, the critical point is a local minimum.
- If $f''(x_0) < 0$, the critical point is a local maximum.
- If $f''(x_0) = 0$, the test is inconclusive.

11. Consider $x_0 = 0$ in the following graphs. In each graph, $f''(0) = 0$.

    (a) Indicate whether the slope of $f(x)$ at $x_0 = 0$ is either zero or non-zero.
    (b) For each graph, identify the type of point at $x_0 = 0$ from the following options. Select all types that apply.

    A. Minimum
    B. Maximum
    C. Critical Point
    D. Inflection Point
    E. None of the above

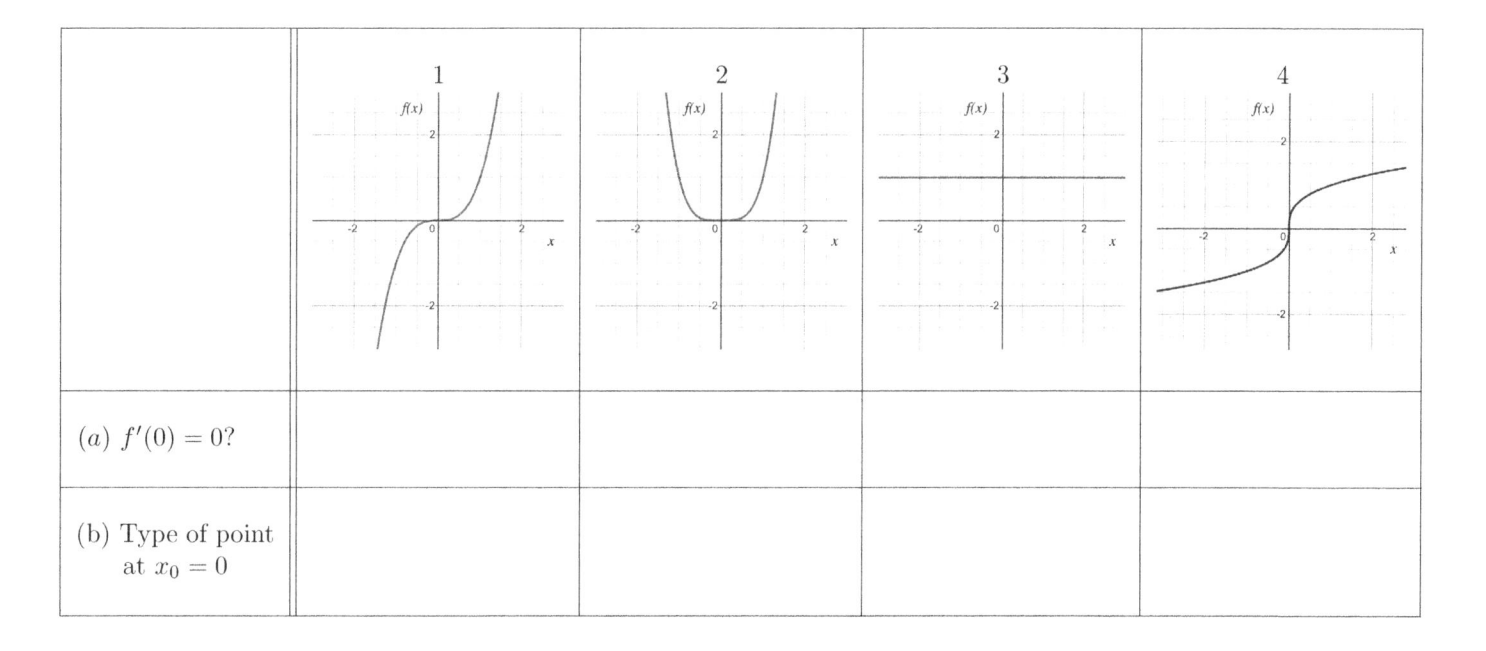

	1	2	3	4
(a) $f'(0) = 0$?				
(b) Type of point at $x_0 = 0$				

Made in the USA
Coppell, TX
19 September 2023